The Debt-Free Teacher

A Complete Guide to Eliminating Debts on Minimal Salary

By Zach Gilliam

Debt-Free Education
www.debtfreeteacher.com

Debt-Free Teacher
How to Live Happy, Follow Your Dreams, Turn Ideas Into Reality

1. Personal Finance 2. Self-Help 3.Educational
www.debtfreeteacher.com

Cover photo by Zach Gilliam
ISBN Print: 978-1-7330568-1-6
ISBN eBook: 978-1-7330568-0-9

Disclaimer:

I want to thank all of the people who have helped me along this journey. Special thanks to Jack Simon, Darcie Finch, Jordan Rodgers, Damon Cathey, and my mother, Laurie Wild, for inspiring me.

I want to dedicate this book to all of my past and future students You can do anything you put your mind to. Everything is possible. Be the light. Be the change you want to see in our world.

Contents

1 My Story.. 1

2 Mindset Mapping 5

3 Growth Mindset.. 11

4 Get Going 16

5 Money Assessment 21

6 Expense Eliminator.. 24

7 Income Increaser... 30

8 Budgeting Blueprint 34

9 Crisis Cash 38

10 Strategic System.. 40

11 Massive Action!.. 45

Resources... 46

Student Loans... 53

Contact 55

1
My Story

I first knew I wanted to teach when I was about 10. My stepmother was a 4th-grade teacher in inner-city Memphis. Her students were victims of poverty, immersed in crime, and had few positive role models in their lives. She kept in touch with her students as they grew into young men and women. She used to visit some students in jail and let them know they could still turn their lives around. Sadly, she attended a few funerals for kids she once called students. I've also had to do this.

The bond between my stepmother and her students was that of a mother and child. She loved and provided for them, often giving rides or buying meals and clothes. Her compassion, as with many teachers, was selfless and second to none. I witnessed a lack of appreciation, embarrassing financial reimbursement, and emotional struggles every day. As I became an educator, those observations grew into my reality. Though there are a million difficulties in the education profession, there are a million more rewards.

My story isn't unique. It's one shared between tens of thousands of people all around the world. I am a public university graduate turned educator living paycheck to paycheck with zero savings and a mountain of student loan debt. Although the specifics may vary from person to person, we all made poor decisions somewhere that led us to taking on debt. That's why we are here, together.

During college, I signed my life away in student loans. I wanted to be intentional about focusing on school, unlike high school, so I used much of my loans to pay things like rent and other living expenses. That wasn't my brightest idea, but it made sense at the time. Although I didn't depend solely on loans, it sure as hell feels that way. Throughout my college years, I cut yards, raked leaves, waited tables, hung Christmas lights, served as a barista, and played in a rock n roll band that seemed to consume money rather than make it. Essentially, I did any odd job that would make beer money.

Post college, I entered the profession carrying a whopping $48,000 of student loan debt. I know for a fact that number reaches into six figures with some educators, especially those who attended graduate programs. Besides my student loans, I found my way into a smaller sum of credit card debt before acquiring a car loan.

After a few years of teaching in the public school system, I had some car issues from my old college clunker, a 2000 Ford Taurus Wagon. That was the second car that bit the dust in a matter of 3 years. At the time, the public transportation system in Nashville was centralized, meaning all routes had to go downtown before connecting to a different part of the city. Geographically, my house and work were separated by the Cumberland River, which has only two crossing points within 5 miles. Not only did the route only run once every hour, but it would have taken over 2 hours to move 20 miles. The Nashville public transportation system was not a viable choice for me, so I rode a bike to work.

Finally, I found a great deal on a decent used car for just under $10k. That kind of money sure as hell wasn't sitting in my bank account. I wanted to get a car that was dependable but could also be used to drive for a rideshare service to make a little money on the side. I went to my bank to get a $10,000 car loan. After filling out an application and having a brief discussion with the bank teller, she came back and said, "Mr. Gilliam, your debt to income ratio is too substantial and your request has been denied."

Somehow, I had managed to get a $20,000 car loan while I was in college making jack shit, but now that I went to college, earned a degree, and worked a full-time public service job, I couldn't get a loan for half of that amount. Plus, I always paid the minimum requirement or overpaid my monthly statements on every loan. I felt defeated, livid, and hopeless. I walked out of the bank, sat in my car and decided that it was time to get serious about getting out of debt.

Since then, I have devoted my future to helping teachers get out of debt. This book and the www.debtfreeteacher.com course were created by a teacher for teachers, but the general concepts can be applied to anyone in any profession. Both will guide you step-by-step through the same process I used to eliminate $32,000 of debt (60k collectively) and save over $15,000 in just 18 months. I recommend reading this book and completing the online course simultaneously to get the full value of Debt-Free Teacher. Make sure that you join the Debt-Free Teachers Facebook group. Those who purchase the online course will receive access to the private network with livestreams and coaching from myself.

This book is a collection of concepts that I have learned from reading many books, watching endless hours of YouTube, and listening to too many podcasts. I am not Dave Ramsey, Mr.

Money Mustache, or any other giant financial guru. I <u>AM</u> a Debt-Free Teacher who wants to share these amazing resources, proven techniques, and strategic approaches to support you in your journey to becoming debt-free.

2
Mindset Mapping

In this section, you will

- ❏ Understand the differences between growth and fixed mindsets
- ❏ Evaluate your current mindset using the DFT Mindset Mapping Tool

During the 2018-2019 school year, the district I was teaching for pushed professional development classes focused on this term called "mindset". I must have attended 4 different PD's and they all presented the concept of understanding and developing mindsets first. This made me think, "Why is everyone talking about mindsets? What's the big deal? Isn't it just the way we think about things?" A few months after the sessions, I realized that I had been using the power of mindset for some time. Not in a classroom context, but, in a financial context. When I built this course, I retraced the steps I took to become debt-free and found that building a growth mindset was the first.

Let's backtrack real quick for contextual purposes. I was teaching a Title I middle school with nearly 90% of the population on free and reduced meals. Our students struggled from an overwhelming amount of hardships every single day. We were on an academic watchlist and identified as a high-risk school for suicide, partially, due to a domino effect from the suicide of one student back in 2015. That school year was the most difficult one of all, but it made me realize how precious life is and how great of an impact students can have on teachers and vice versa.

Just before the 2018-2019 school year started, I had a dream that led me to the question, "How am I going to get these kids to grow?" Between low academic performance, major behavioral problems, and a toxic culture, it felt like a David and Goliath scenario. I needed a simple approach. So I started with the acronym G.R.O.W. We needed to "G.R.O.W." as a class, staff, and school.

G is for Greatness. To grow, we must be great. Great at what? Great at everything we do. Great in our attitudes and mindsets. Great in our homework assignments or interactions with coworkers. Students must challenge themselves and their actions should reflect greatness. I must be a great teacher for my students and uplift them, hold them accountable for their actions, and lead by example. We must show up to school every day and be great for our community.

R is for "Ready". If we are going to grow, we must be ready. I can't show up to school not knowing what I will teach that day and expect my results to be amazing. Students can't show up to class without a pencil and paper or the previous night's homework assignment and expect to make gains in a class they're struggling with. We must commit to being ready for growth in all areas of our lives.

O is for "Optimistic". If you wake up telling yourself today going to be a horrible day, it probably will be. If I walk into the classroom and say, "These students are too low to complete grade level tasks. There's no way I can grow them in "x" amount of time," that becomes my reality. In order to grow, a student has to approach academic hardships with a yet mentality: "I'm not sure how to solve proportions, yet. I'm not sure I know how to set up this word problem, yet." We must look for the "glass half full" at all times.

W is for the "WOW factor". What can you do to "WOW" someone today? The wow factor means going out of your way to help others, even if it's inconvenient. It's stopping to help a coworker who is carrying too many things. It's holding the door for the students we "love the most". It's asking questions and letting someone know that you care. Basically, anything you can do to make someone say or think "wow".

I went to a P.D. on the 7 Habits of Highly Effective People the morning after I created the G.R.O.W. acronym. I was so pumped that I shared it with our numeracy coach, Dr. Darcie Finch, who has always been an inspiration to me. Later in the PD, she asked me to share it with everyone on the microphone. I felt a little nervous, but confident in the purpose. It was amazing to see how many teachers actually connected with that message. Our 7th-grade team loved it so much, we incorporated it as our motto for the year. If you walked down the 7th-grade hall or in my classroom, you saw giant letters on the windows that said G.R.O.W. As I developed Debt-Free Teacher, I realized that "G.R.O.W." was a mindset. A mindset that pushes us to be our best selves.

Mindsets have been around since the beginning of time, but we didn't coin the term until the 1930s. There are many variations of mindsets out there that are used throughout different contexts. World-renowned researcher of mindsets, Carol Dweck, is a professor of Psychology at Stanford University that has focused her research on fostering success and understanding why people succeed. Much of the information we will cover comes from her book, *Mindset: The New Psychology of Success*. I highly recommend giving it a read.

Mindsets are the way people think about ability and talent. "It's a simple idea that makes all the difference. There are two types of mindsets: fixed and growth. It's essential to define and identify the characteristics of both mindsets to establish a foundation that will sustain building the habits you need to get out of debt.

In a fixed mindset, people believe their basic qualities, like their intelligence or talent, are simply fixed traits. They spend their time documenting their intelligence or talent instead of developing them. They also believe that talent alone creates success—without effort.

In a growth mindset, people believe that their most basic abilities can be developed through dedication and hard work—brains and talent are just the starting point. Failure is viewed as an opportunity to learn. This view creates a love of learning and a resilience essential for great accomplishment. Teaching a growth mindset will enhance relationships, motivation, and productivity.

Let's take a look at the responses of teachers with different mindsets. "How am I supposed to get out of debt on a teacher's salary?"

Fixed mindset responses may include:	**Growth mindsets** response may include:
-It's impossible. -There isn't any way to get out of (your amount) debt with a teacher's salary. -Living expenses are too high and there's no room for extra cash flow. -I can't even make the minimum payments. -How do you expect me to get out of debt when I don't have enough time to get another job and I can't make any more money teaching?	-I'm not sure how, but I will give it everything I've got. -I'm not debt-free, yet. -I can do anything if I put my mind to it. -I'm tired of feeling trapped. -I will be free from all forms of debt! -I can do this! Yes, I can. -I decide my future!

Which mindset do you have? Some teachers believe they have a strong growth mindset when they actually have a fixed mindset with some growth ideas. Stop what you're doing right now and use the DFT Mindset Mapping Tool to determine your current mindset. It will give you a better idea of where you stand on the mindset spectrum. Complete the Mindset Map survey to determine your current mindset.

www.debtfreeteacher.com/mindsetmaptool

Action Steps
1. Complete the Mindset Mapping Tool 2. Be Honest and Transparent

3

Growth Mindset

In this section you will

❑ Cultivate and sustain a debt-free mindset
❑ Change fixed notions into growth notions

Now, you have completed the Mindset Map. Let's analyze your results. Does your current mindset lean more towards a growth mindset, a fixed mindset, or a mixture of both? So now what? Acknowledge your current mindset and be open to new opportunities.

"Whether you can or you can't, you're right."
-Unknown Author

Not too long ago, I was at the park playing basketball with another teacher. I jumped as high as I could and made a lay up. My friend said, "You can dunk, right?" I started to say, "Ya right, I can't dunk", but I stopped myself and said, "I can dunk, I just haven't yet!" No isn't a part of the growth mindset vocabulary. When we tell ourselves that we can't do something, we are right. At that moment, we have professed our futures.

We must transition to using language that promotes our successes. The more we use growth language, the more it becomes part of our reality. Dweck created a 4-step process to help us cultivate a growth mindset or to continue fostering a growth mindset.

1. Learn to hear your fixed mindset "voice."

As you approach a challenge, that voice might say to you "Are you sure you can do it? Maybe you don't have the talent." "What if you fail—you'll be a failure." "People will laugh at you for thinking you had talent." "If you don't try, you can protect yourself and keep your dignity."

As you hit a setback, the voice might say, "This would have been a snap if you really had talent." "You see, I told you it was a risk. Now you've gone and shown the world how limited you are." "It's not too late to back out, make excuses, and try to regain your dignity."

As you face criticism, you might hear yourself say, "It's not my fault. It was something or someone else's fault." You might feel yourself getting angry at the person who is giving you feedback. "Who do they think they are? I'll put them in their place." The other person might be giving you specific, constructive feedback, but you might be hearing them say "I'm really disappointed in you. I thought you were capable but now I see you're not."

2. Recognize that you have a choice.

How you interpret challenges, setbacks, and criticism is YOUR CHOICE! You can interpret them in a fixed mindset as signs that your fixed talents or abilities are lacking. Or you can interpret them in a growth mindset as signs you need to ramp up your strategies and effort, stretch yourself, and expand your abilities. It's up to you.

So as you face challenges, setbacks, and criticism throughout this course, listen to the fixed mindset voice and use step 3.

3. Talk back to it with a growth mindset voice.

<u>*As you approach a challenge:*</u>

THE FIXED-MINDSET says,	THE GROWTH-MINDSET answers,
"Are you sure you can do it? Maybe you don't have the talent."	*"I'm not sure I can do it YET, but I think I can learn to with time and effort."*
"What if you fail—you'll be a failure"	*"Most successful people had failures along the way."*
"If you don't try, you can protect yourself and keep your dignity."	*"If I don't try, I automatically fail. Where's the dignity in that?"*

As you hit a setback:

FIXED MINDSET:	GROWTH MINDSET:
"This would have been a snap if you really had talent."	"That is so wrong. Basketball wasn't easy for Michael Jordan and science wasn't easy for Thomas Edison. They had a passion and put in tons of effort.

As you face criticism:

FIXED MINDSET:	GROWTH MINDSET:
"It's not my fault. It was something or someone else's fault."	"If I don't take responsibility, I can't fix it. Let me listen—however painful it is, and learn whatever I can."

Then...

4. Take the growth mindset action.
Over time, which voice you heed becomes your choice. Whether you

> _take on the challenge wholeheartedly,_
> _learn from your setbacks and try again_
> _hear the criticism and act on it is now in your hands._

Practice hearing both voices, and practice acting on the growth mindset. See how you can make it work for you.

After you practice incorporating a growth mindset, you will recognize vast quantities of fixed traits within our culture. Just turn on the television or scroll through your news feed. Even the school and the teacher's lounge can be a toxic environment. These are all part of the obstacles you must overcome daily.

Don't let the clutter bring you down. Don't let someone else's words or opinions bring you down. It is truly your choice! Choose to grow and push yourself to be the greatest person you can be. The next chapter will move mountains and help you overcome any hurdles that lie ahead. Follow these action steps. Seriously, follow these action steps. Be intentional about incorporating them into your daily practices.

Action Steps

1. **Practice Cultivating and Sustaining a Growth Mindset**
    a. **Learn to hear your "fixed" voice**
    b. **Recognize you have a choice**
    c. **Respond with a "growth" voice**
    d. **Take Growth action**
2. **Stop telling yourself "You can't" or "It's impossible"**
3. **Practice viewing all failures and obstacles as learning opportunities**

4

Get Going

In this section, you will

- ❑ Let go of preconceived notions
- ❑ Understand the power of affirmations
- ❑ Create affirmations of your own to practice
- ❑ Acquire an Accountabilibuddy

To transform our current financial status, we need to apply our understanding of a growth mindset to our lifestyle. This means **letting go** of previous notions that say, "This is my current situation and I can't do anything about it." and **let's go** to financial independence and gain a debt-free lifestyle you control.

A friend once told me, "Our minds are our hardware. What we install in them is our software. There are all types of bugs and viruses out there, so we need to be careful when deciding what software to install." We have the freedom to install any software (mindset) we want. If you chose to consume negative media and surround yourself with people that do the same, those are the results you'll get. If you choose to consume positive content and surround yourself with people that encourage and inspire others, those are the results you will get. If you want to succeed in your debt-free journey, you must start with affirmations.

I continually recite positive affirmations out loud daily. It's amazing how many people have thanked me for the inspiration. Affirmations are carefully created statements crafted around positive thinking and self-empowerment. They use the power of positive mentality to accomplish success in anything. For affirmations to be fruitful, they should be positive, specific, personalized, and used in the present tense.

Scan over this list of affirmations and pick a few that stand out or mean something to you. Add some of your own affirmations if they motivate and inspire you. I want you to record a voice memo on your phone saying the affirmations like you truly believe them. Listen to these affirmations when you wake up, on the way to work, when you're brushing your teeth, or any spare moment you have. The more you listen, the more you actually say these things without the recording. You are programming your mindset! This is a necessity for a successful debt-free journey!

"Letting Go" and "Let's Go" Affirmations

-I am on my way to financial freedom!

- -I will be debt-free!
- -I can do anything I put my mind to!
- -Can't Never Could!
- -I am an amazing educator!
- -I acknowledge the blessings I have received in my life with gratitude, I feel honored and humbled.
- -Everything I desire in life is in front of me.
- -Success and good fortune flow toward me in a river of abundance.
- -I am grateful for each day that brings me one step closer to my perfect life.

- -I control my future.
- -I am extremely confident in anything that I do.
- -I feel heroic, confident and exhilarated.
- -I know my actions today will create momentum tomorrow and the next day - I feel unstoppable.
- -The future is mine. I have only to claim it.
- -I welcome freedom into my mind, I am not restrained to anything and can do whatever I want. I feel free and empowered.
- -I refuse to let debt control my life.
- -I will be a debt-free teacher!

During your path to becoming debt-free, you must acquire an "account-a-bila-buddy". An accountabilibuddy is someone holds you accountable for your actions. This can be a spouse, family member, coworker, friend, or fellow teacher. There is more power in having an accountabilibuddy in the teaching field because they truly understand your situation and identify with the struggles that come with teaching.

Consider the following when choosing an accountabilibuddy:

- Don't just pick anyone. Pick someone accomplished in an area and can help you grow.
- You can have more than one accountability partner for various things.
- Your accountabilibuddy can be anywhere in the world thanks to technology. Use Skype, FaceTime, or something similar.
- Figure out what type of communication works best (text, phone call, in person, or a mix)
- Schedule routine communication with this person. Put it in your calendar! Set an alarm. This can be the same time every week or switch it.
- Prepare in advance. Make notes of things you want to discuss or goals you want to accomplish and send it to them. This way both of you can jump right in when you meet up.
- Be honest and transparent. If you don't, you'll just be wasting everyone's time.

The goal here is for someone or some people to hold you accountable for fighting the debt-free fight. An accountabilibuddy that doesn't hold you accountable is **cheating your success**. Ditch them and find a new one. If you're having trouble finding one, contact the Debt-Free Teacher Private Facebook group. There are thousands of other teachers going through the exact same thing. I built the group just for this! We are here for you!

These action steps create the foundation that you're building your debt-free lifestyle on. Do not cheat yourself!

Part 1: Action Steps

1. Acquire an accountabilibuddy
   a. Schedule Check-in's
   b. Come prepared
   c. Relay goals to them
   d. Be honest and transparent
2. Choose personal affirmations
3. Record an audio file of your affirmations
4. Listen to and repeat your affirmations every day. Those words become your reality when you listen/repeat your affirmations often.

5
Money Assessment

In this section, you will:

- Understand the importance of tracking your money

As teachers, we are already at a disadvantage. Teaching is one of the most overworked, underappreciated, and underpaid professions in the world. We should know where every single penny is coming from and going to. It's silly for us to sit around and complain about the cards WE chose when we knew these things coming into the profession. It's not a secret. This isn't a new discovery. Teachers have struggled with these things since the late 18th century. We have to tell our money where to go!

The Financial Industry Regulatory Authority found that more than a third of the population would not be able to sustain a $2,000 emergency bill in the next month. That covers things like broken down cars or major house repairs. These figures were extremely high for people without college degrees (81%), those with an income of less than $25,000, and African Americans (48%). The Debt-Free Teacher course works to eliminate such statistics beginning with setting up a budget. Later on, we will use the DFT Budgeting Blueprint to categorize your expenses and incomes to create an effective budget.

You must focus on building your wealth gap in order to get out of debt. A wealth gap is the distance between our income and expenses. The smaller our wealth gap is, the harder it is to keep our head above water. Some wealth gaps may even be inverted, where your expenses are greater than your income. This doesn't mean anything is impossible, but it will require more effort to get on the right path. The larger our wealth gap is, the more freedom we have.

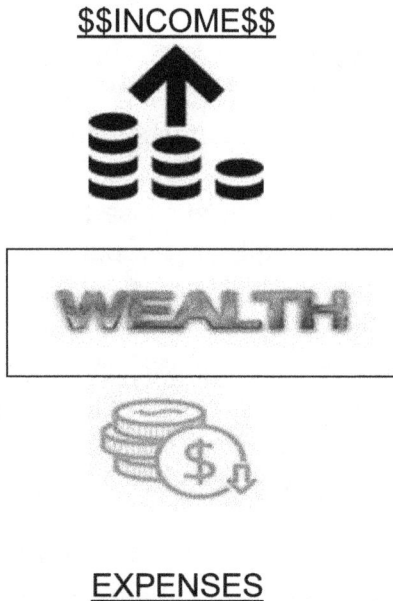

$$INCOME$$

WEALTH

EXPENSES

There are only two ways to expand our wealth gaps: decrease our expenses and increase our income. We will achieve our financial goals much faster when we increase our income streams and eliminate/decrease expenses. The next few chapters will help you make gains in expanding this gap in both directions.

Action Steps
1. Ask yourself, "Do I know where every penny went last month?"
2. "Do I know exactly how much money I am making?"

6
Expense Eliminator

In this section, you will

- ❏ Track your expenses
- ❏ Categorize your expenses
- ❏ Eliminate some expenses
- ❏ Gain Additional Resources for Student Loan Debt

Starting now, I want you to keep track of every penny you spend. There are plenty of money tracking apps in the app store on your phone. I prefer to order pocket-sized notebooks off Amazon and carry them with me. There's something about physically writing each expense down that helps me feel more connected to this process. Record each expense the moment you pay it. When the waiter drops the bill off, record it. When you check out at the grocery, record it before you walk out the door. I love it when friends or bystanders comment and ask questions when I'm filling out my expenses. I've heard things like, "You're serious, aren't you? Do you record everything? Wow, that's dedication. That's awesome!" I feel motivated each time someone says something. Half the time, they're the same people complaining about not having enough money.

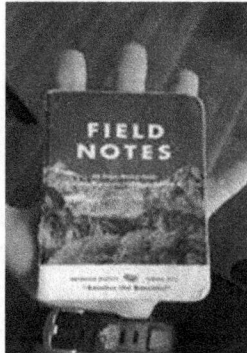

One of my pocket books.

First, we must look at expenses. Simplify put, an expense is money spent. Expenses would include things like rent, transportation, entertainment, subscriptions, credit cards, student loans, mortgage, cell phone bills, utilities, food, and so on. It is essential that you list out all of the money you spend monthly. You'll need to fetch your bank account statements for the last three months and a scratch sheet of paper to help you do this. Divide your expenses into 2 categories on your sheet of paper.

NEEDS	Totals	Wants	Totals
Rent/Mortgage	$760	Netflix	$14.99

The first category is **"needs"**, as they are necessary for day-to-day living. Think to yourself, "What do I need to live this month/year?" Obviously, things like food and shelter come to mind, but don't forget about things like transportation, toiletries, and insurance. Think bare bone, bare necessities, no fluff when listing your needs. Do not list things like "going to the movies twice a month to see the latest flick" on this list. Be brutally honest with yourself. We are stripping your expenses down to what you need to survive day-to-day. Go ahead and list all of your needs.

Next on the expense list are the **"wants"**. Wants are things that will not affect our overall well-being if we do not have them. Some examples of "wants" are Netflix, subscriptions, shopping, concerts, clothing (in the name of fashion), gifts, going to athletic events, or getting those Girl Scout cookies when they post up in front of the grocery store. Most things we encounter will fall under the "wants" category. Wants are tied to our emotions, not our financial well-being. Go ahead and list all of your wants.

Now that you have divided your expenses, let's work on expanding your wealth gap. Remember, our wealth gap is the distance between our income and expenses. We must start by decreasing our expenses. The more expenses we can eliminate or decrease, the faster we will achieve our financial goals. Know that your actions today will create momentum for tomorrow and the next day. You must cut your expenses. It's time to dig deep and make sacrifices. Say goodbye to wants and cut your needs when possible. Here are a few ideas to start you. Be creative and think outside the box.

Transportation	Take public transportation more often; walking, biking, or scooter; carpool; host events instead of attending,
Food	STOP EATING OUT; go to the grocery store (Save-a-lot, Aldi not Whole Foods); beans and rice diet; Remember the Ramen Noodles from college? Buy in large quantities; use coupons;
Shopping	Second Hand/Thrift Stores: do you really need it? ;
Going Out	Host friends; drop or at least cut back on the expensive alcoholic drinks; stop going to boujee restaurants and bars; don't get the prime rib, get the kids meal;
Miscellaneous	Cancel subscriptions, attend free events; borrow books from the library instead of buying them

Remember, we want to use the growth mindset to its fullest potential. That means believing in the process when you're listing and cutting your wants and needs. Believe that transparency and honesty with yourself will lead you into freedom of debt eventually. Let's do this!

Finally, the topic we've all been waiting for: student loans. According to the Debt-Free Education survey, 87.5% of teachers have student loan debt. When I left college, I had $48k of student loan debt, and that's pennies compared to some teachers I coach. Loan forgiveness programs are a partial solution, but they aren't guaranteed and may change depending on current presidential administrations.

Use these resources to guide you through the ins and outs of student loan forgiveness. The best part is that no other profession has this many loan forgiveness programs. Some programs can be combined but not used at the same time. For instance, if you use the Teacher Loan Forgiveness Program (TLFP) after 5 years, you could then apply for Public Service Loan Forgiveness (PSLF) after an additional 10 years. This makes little sense because PSLF forgives the entire amount after 10 years. So, if you're considering this option, just go with the PSLF.

If you have decided that you didn't want to teach any longer, you may choose the TLFP instead because the duration is only 5 years. Also, it could make sense if you haven't consolidated your loans and have Federal Family Education Loans (FFEL). Since FFEL loans don't qualify for PSLF, you could do Teacher Loan Forgiveness first, then consolidate your loans and go for PSLF.

Teacher Loan Forgiveness Program (TLFP)
I used this program to eliminate $17,500 of debt! That's almost $20k taken off just for meeting their criteria. Educators must teach Math, Science, or SPED in a low-income based school (Title I) for 5 consecutive years to qualify. The program forgives $5,000-$17,500 depending on the grade level and if you are "highly qualified" or not. Once you have completed 5 years, you can apply for forgiveness.

Public Service Loan Forgiveness | Federal Student Aid
PSLF is one of the best ways to receive loan forgiveness. Teachers can receive complete Federal student loan forgiveness after 120 qualifying payments (10 yrs). This program is awesome because it applies to any teacher at any school.

Perkins Loan Cancellation and Discharge | Federal Student Aid
If you have Perkins Loans, you can see your entire loan balance forgiven over 5 years. The great thing about this program is that it gives forgiveness in increments, so even if you don't make it 5 years, you can at least see some of your loan balance disappear. Private schools can be eligible. You must teach math, science, foreign language, bilingual studies, and any other content area determined to be in shortage in your state.

State-Based Student Loan Forgiveness Programs
There are a plethora of state-based student loan forgiveness programs. Each state is unique and some states have no programs at all. You can find this information, see if your school qualifies, and more details about each program at
https://debtfreeteacher.com/resources/

Action Steps
1. Track every penny you spend. Use an app on your phone or a pocket-sized notebook.
2. Divide your expenses into wants and needs.
3. Find ways to decrease the money you are spending on needs.
4. Eliminate and/or decrease money spend on wants.

7
Income Increaser

In this section, you will

- ❑ Things I did to raise my income
- ❑ Learn when and how to increase your income
- ❑ Resources/Ideas

Income is money received. We should start by incorporating recurring monthly income. This is income you receive regularly. If teaching is your only gig, then you should list your typical paycheck.

As the whole world knows, teaching is an underpaid profession. That's half the reason you're here. Breaks and holidays are some of the most sought-after components of teaching, so we will use them to our advantage. As teachers, we anticipate breaks just as much if not more than students.

During my 18-month journey to tackling debt, I gave up almost all of my breaks minus Thanksgiving and Christmas days. It sounds kind of crazy, but I was determined to get out of debt. When I was a kid, I used to run from my parents before a spanking and my dad would say, "might as well get it over with."

That's your mentality until all debts are gone. Remember, sacrifices now will mean complete freedom in the future!

The summer before I was completely debt-free, I worked my ass off cutting the neighbors grass, driving pedicabs (bicycle cab), working in a local bicycle shop on the weekends, driving Uber, charging Bird and Lime scooters, tuning up bikes by word of mouth, selling things I didn't use. Literally any opportunity to make more money, I did it and you will too.

You **NEED** to find ways to increase your income after work, on the weekends, or any other time you can find. If you have children this could be more difficult, but it's not impossible. You must be creative. Could you and your spouse alternate watching the kids? Maybe you're involved in a church with a youth group that meets two nights a week. Do you have trusted family or friends that might help out every now and then? Grandparents love this part! Check into before and after-school programs offered at your child's school.

If you don't have time to make extra income, then you don't have time to Netflix, surf social media, or go to the movies. So many of us will swear that we don't have a minute of time to spare, but yet, we just spent an hour surfing Facebook. Make time and sacrifices now or you'll continue to live a life of debt. Remember, fixed mindsets say we can't and growth mindsets say we can. Again, you must be creative. Even if it's just one or two days a week, make it happen.

So let's look at some things you can do for extra income. Naturally, teachers are good at teaching. Use your talents and certifications to teach or tutor online. There are a few reputable tutoring websites and teaching opportunities. Check out www.debtfreeteacher.com/resources for an extensive list of extra income opportunities for teacher schedules. Also, put up tutoring flyers at the YMCA, local community centers, libraries, and social media.

There may be coaching opportunities available in your district and possibly your school. These positions are usually decided at the beginning of the year, so act accordingly. Once, I served as head basketball coach at my school, even though I had no clue what I was doing. We went 2-10 that year. It wasn't pretty, but I used that income to repay student loans and was about $3,000 closer to becoming debt-free. The good thing is that there's a sport for every season. Use Google and YouTube religiously. The bad thing is sports can be very time-consuming. Before accepting a position, consult with another coach and consider the time the eligibility and behavioral components take up.

During the 2017-2018 school year, I worked on the Scope and Sequence Revision Team for my district and made a good chunk of change I normally wouldn't have. Stay up to date with everything going on at school and your district. You may find one-off earning opportunities. If you do, take them!

Next, consider things you are already good at or may have an existing connection to. I have a fair amount of knowledge and experience with bicycles, so I reached out to the owner of a local bike shop and picked up some weekend shifts.

Then there are things like Uber, Lyft, Bird, Lime, and quite a few other companies (also listed on the RESOURCES page) that outsource work to contracted employees. They allow you to work when you are ready. I recommend doing a bit of research to find the secrets to capitalizing your income and using your time wisely. There is a method to the madness, so don't give up if you aren't killing it immediately. Anything that is increasing your income is a step in the right direction.

INCOME IDEAS

Charge scooters, tutor, additional teaching opportunities, recycling, Uber/Lyft, teach English to foreign students online, create content for Teacherspayteachers.com or any other similar website, bartend, Rover app, pet sitting/walking apps, donate plasma, wash cars, cut lawns, rake leaves, babysit, drop shipping, make YouTube videos, social media content, become an affiliate for your favorite websites (Ebay, Amazon are great!), house cleaning, clean Airbnbs, Airbnb, VRBO, Flipkey, HomeAway, Homestay, paid online surveys, rent your car out using Turo, Sell the gift cards you never used online, sell things you aren't using around the house or up in the attic. Think Craigslist or FB Marketplace, garage sale, use your talent (photography, teaching, music, graphic design, sewing, etc.). There are thousands of ways to make more money while maintaining a full-time teaching position.

Action Steps

1. **Increase your income. Be creative.**
2. **Utilize my "Resources" to find income opportunities.**
3. **Stop wasting your free time doing things that don't increase your income!**
4. **Start NOW!**

8

Budgeting Blueprint

In this section, you will

- ❏ Organize your expenses and income into the DFT Budgeting Tool
- ❏ Set Monthly and Weekly Budgets
- ❏ Rare Expenses
- ❏ Extra Money

*Head on over to
www.debtfreeteacher.com/budgetingblueprinttool to access the Budgeting Blueprint Tool.

The Budgeting Blueprint tool is one of the most valuable resources of this course. If used correctly, it can change your life. The whole purpose here is to strategically organize your debts, expenses, and income so you can find gains to apply to your outstanding balances. The blueprint has built-in formulas that will do the work for you. If you need extra assistance, post it in our Debt-Free Teachers FB group.

By now, you have pinpointed where you can decrease your expenses, categorized your expenses, and increased your income stream. Now, let's put them to work. Enter the average into your Budgeting Blueprint. List each need in both the monthly and yearly categories. If you pay $73 for your cell phone each month, find the yearly cost by multiplying 12 x $73 for a total of $876.

	Monthly Expense	Yearly Expense
Cell Phone	$73	$876

Notice the Debt Diagram function within the Budgeting Blueprint. Don't worry about filling in this portion just yet. We will get to it in the Strategic System portion of the course.

After you plug in your information into the blueprint, it's time to set up a budget. A budget is just an estimate of income and expenditure for a set period. You should have 3 budgets: weekly, monthly, and yearly. Using cash and envelopes is the best way for weekly budgets because you can physically tell if there's any surplus money or if your funds have run out. I spent all of my cash before the end of the week for the first few weeks of budgeting but started having surplus money after I got the hang of it.

My weekly budget is basic. I have three categories: gas, groceries, and entertainment. Everything else (rent, cell phone, insurance, etc.) is set on automatic payments online. If the expense is not gas or groceries, I use my entertainment envelope to cover the cost. When I go out to eat, that money comes from entertainment. Call your categories whatever you want but keep it simple. For a single person living in a bustling city on a teacher's salary, I budgeted $150/160 cash every week. Most weeks, I have excess money from gas and entertainment. I was only able to make a $40 grocery budget because of Aldi. Aldi cut my grocery bill in half.

<u>My Weekly Budget</u>
Gas- $40
Groceries - $40
Entertainment - $80

Monthly budgets should include everything it takes for you to live that month. Account for mortgage/rent, loans, utilities, and anything else you can think of. You need not take cash out for this, but be mindful and try to set up auto pay for things that only come once a month. Plug your numbers into the Yearly Glance tab and each individual month as you progress through the system.

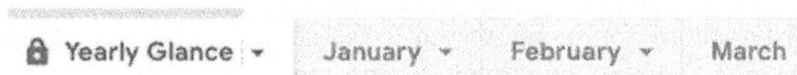

🔒 Yearly Glance ▾   January ▾   February ▾   March

Use the budgeting blueprint to calculate your annual totals. This is your annual budget. The blueprint will calculate what percentage of your annual income each category takes up. This can also help you identify places you should make cuts. For example, if you're spending 35% of your annual income on a car (insurance, maintenance) note that you should consider getting a different car.

What about the "one-off" expenses that happen in life. Things that don't come around every week or month. The Yearly Glance tab accounts for rare expenses like oil changes, tires, haircuts, and more. Prepare for these expenses in advance and you won't be scrambling when the mechanic comes back and says that you need a new set of tires or a new alternator.

Remember, we don't want to fight debt with debt, but rather be ready with cash in hand.

After you get the hang of your budget, lower your expenses, and increase your income, you will have extra cash. You can find this in the upper right-hand corner of the blueprint. We'll dive deeper into how to use that money in the next chapter.

Action Steps
1. Organize all of your expenses and income into the Budgeting Blueprint.
2. Create weekly, monthly, and annual budgets.
3. Pull out "x" cash at the beginning of each week. When it's gone, it's gone.
4. Continue to record every penny you spend.

9

Crisis Cash

In this section, you will

☐ Know the 4 W's of Crisis Cash

What?

The first part of the Strategic System is to save up Crisis Cash of $1500. If you don't already have $1,500 saved, this will be your number one priority. Crisis Cash is ONLY for emergencies. You should never touch this fund unless it's an absolute emergency. If your car breaks down and it's your only mode of transportation, use the Crisis Cash. If your AC goes out in the middle of summer, use your Crisis Cash. If tickets just went on sale for your favorite band, dream about how awesome it will be to see them once you are out of debt, but don't touch your Crisis Cash!

Why?

Because life happens and we must be prepared for it. Fighting debt with debt is a horrible idea that only digs a deeper hole that's harder to get out of. Our ultimate goal is to eliminate our debts to create freedom. This makes me think of natural disasters. Growing up, my dad was into storm shelters. My memory is vague, but I think he may have sold them for a little while. They are massive ventilated structures that people bury underground in case of a tornado or natural disaster. If you live in "Tornado Alley" you know what I'm talking about.

People store large amounts of nonperishable foods and water inside, along with games and anything else that might come in handy. When a tornado comes, they seek shelter inside. Even if the disaster destroyed everything in the area, they are safe, secure, and prepared. This is the equivalent of Crisis Cash.

When?

This is the first part of setting up your strategic system. It's kind of like crawling before you walk. Make this your number one priority and do it now! The faster you create this fund, the faster you will be out of debt.

Where?

Subtract your expenses from your income to figure out how much "extra cash" you have left each month. This is the bright green box in the upper right-hand corner of your budgeting blueprint. This is where you will get the money to build up your Crisis Cash and the money for your strategy. It's okay if it's a small amount. Something is better than nothing.

Your crisis cash doesn't necessarily have to be cash. Store it somewhere you won't be tempted to use it. It's probably not a good idea to store it in a checking account. Keep it safely hidden in your house, or better yet, in a secure savings account.

Action Steps
1. Use your "extra cash" to build a $1500 Crisis Cash Fund. 2. Start now!

10
Strategic System

In this section, you will

- ❏ Compare Snowball vs. Avalanche
- ❏ Order debts

In this segment, I will teach you about two highly effective strategies to eliminate your loans. Both strategies will accomplish the same goal and focus on paying minimums on all debts except for one **focus debt**. After you have your Crisis Cash, send all of your "extra cash" from the Budgeting Blueprint directly to your focus debt. Once each **focus debt** has been paid off, take the money poured into the focus debt and transfer it directly to the next debt in line. The money spent on the focus debt will continually increase because you are pouring the money from the previous focus debt and the minimum from the new focus debt simultaneously.

Many people debate which strategy is the best, but ultimately, it's a matter of personal preference. The biggest difference between them is how you organize your focus debts. The best strategy for paying off debt is whichever one works for you. You must decide which method that is.

The Snowball Strategy

The first method I want to share with you is the Snowball. This method was coined and made famous by the financial guru Dave Ramsey. This is also the method I used to get rid of my $32,000 of debt. The snowball method requires that all debts be ordered from least to greatest. First, begin by sending all of your "extra" money into paying the smallest debt. If you pick up more income throughout the month, it must go into the smallest debt. Once, the smallest debt has been paid in full, take that money and add it to the minimum payment of the next debt. Look at the images. Image 1 reflects the person's minimum payment on their smallest loan is $25, but they are paying $125. This means they found an "extra" $100 a month after budgeting. The entire $100 is paid to the smallest debt until it's paid in full and then transferred to Debt 2.

Image 1

Debt/Interest Rate	Debt 1 ($1,000/4.6%)	Debt 2 ($2,000/3.8%)	Debt 3 ($3,000/5.2%)
Min payment	25.00	50.00	80.00
Actual	$125.00	50	80

Image 2

	Debt 1 ($1,000/4.6%)	Debt 2 ($2,000/3.8%)	Debt 3 ($3,000/5.2%)
Min payment	0.00	50.00	80.00

| Actual | ~~Paid in full~~ | 50 + 125.00 =175.00 | 80 |

Image 2 reflects the $125 that was spent on Debt 1 was added to the minimum payment of Debt 2 ($50). As you can see, the amount that is paid to the smallest loan continually grows as it acquires a new debt ($125 + $50 = $175). This is where the term snowball comes from.

Take note that the interest rates are irrelevant while using this strategy. The snowball method is effective because of all the small wins. Small wins give the debtor a sense of accomplishment and a boost of energy to tackle the next debt in line because they feel successful. The feeling of success is the biggest motivating factor that exists. If you value smaller and faster wins, this strategy is for you.

The Avalanche Strategy

The second strategy is the Avalanche method. The biggest difference between the Snowball and the Avalanche is how debts are ordered. The Avalanche method requires that you tackle your debts from greatest to least by interest rates. Mathematically, the Avalanche is the fastest way to becoming debt-free. Eventually, you will pay back less money and do it faster than if you used the Snowball. Some of you might be thinking, "Why in the hell would someone use the Snowball, if the Avalanche pays less faster?" It goes back to what type of personality you have.

If paying back less money in a shorter amount of time is more important AND you have patience, run with the Avalanche. If smaller motivational wins will help you stay on track for the long run, go with the Snowball. The choice is yours.

It's time to organize your debts into a format that will allow you to prioritize repayments. After you have decided which strategy to use, gather a list of all of your debts. This should include mortgages, student loans, medical bills, credit cards, and anything else you owe money to. Insert the debts into the Debt Diagram on the Budgeting Blueprint based on the strategy you have chosen (Snowball/Avalanche).

List

Creditor	Balance	Rate
Card #3	1,550.00	12.00%
Card #4	2,500.00	16.00%
Card #2	3,500.00	21.00%
Card #1	4,400.00	18.00%
Auto Loan #1	7,750.00	14.00%
Student Loan #2	9,500.00	3.50%
Student Loan #1	11,800.00	4.00%
	41,000.00	

SNOWBALL

Creditor	Balance	Rate
Card #3	1,550.00	12.00%
Card #4	2,500.00	16.00%
Card #2	3,500.00	21.00%
Card #1	4,400.00	18.00%
Auto Loan #1	7,750.00	14.00%
Student Loan #2	9,500.00	3.50%
Student Loan #1	11,800.00	4.00%
	41,000.00	

AVALANCHE

Creditor	Balance	Rate
Card #2	3,500.00	21.00%
Card #1	4,400.00	18.00%
Card #4	2,500.00	16.00%
Auto Loan #1	7,750.00	14.00%
Card #3	1,550.00	12.00%
Student Loan #1	11,800.00	4.00%
Student Loan #2	9,500.00	3.50%
	41,000.00	

After you list your debts and interest rates using the Debt Diagram, it's time to execute the plan.

Action Steps
1. Decide which Strategic System works best for your personality. Choose one and commit.
2. Order your debts into the Debt Diagram on your Budgeting Blueprint.

11
Massive Action!

You've done the legwork, developed a growth mindset, acquired an accountabilibuddy, set goals, budgeted, and decided which strategy to use. Now, it's time to execute the plan. Use your accountabilibuddy for support and advice often. When you hit an obstacle or feel discouraged, refer to the affirmations and 4 steps to cultivating a growth mindset. Use the Crisis Cash if an emergency happens.

Watch your debts disappear and let your chosen Strategic System work for you. Throw all of your extra cash at your focus debt. Ask questions in our Debt-Free Teacher Facebook group. Know your actions today will create momentum tomorrow and the next day. You are unstoppable. Tune in to my live streams. The only difference between you and the life you dream of is action!

If you felt the information in this book was valuable for you, but you are having difficulty executing the plan, let me help you personally. You can apply for one-on-one coaching at www.debtfreeteacher.com/go . I only take on a handful of clients each month, so I can give each person my undivided attention. My goal is to help every teacher become free of debt.

Resources

Visit www.debtfreeteacher.com/resources for live links and updated information. The following resources provide extra income from teaching:

Teachers Pay Teachers
TpT is the go-to place for educators to find the resources, knowledge, and inspiration they need to teach at their best. They offer more than 3 million free and paid resources, created by educators who understand what works in the classroom. Their marketplace is growing every day to meet the evolving needs of the PreK-12 classroom. When educators get the resources and support they need, they're best equipped to inspire our next generation of learners.

VIPKID
VIPKID is linking the world through education by providing an international learning experience that allows you to teach Chinese children from the comfort of your own home.

DADA English – DaDaABC.com
Founded in 2013, DaDa is the leading online English education platform based in China. Since its inception, DaDa's mission is to be the best online international school in China through one-on-one student-teacher pairing, world-class teaching content, and industry-leading two-way interactive learning platform.

DaDa is the proud partner of Pearson Education, McGraw-Hill Education, Oxford University Press, National Geographic Learning, Highlights, and many other prestigious publishers and learning centers.

Qkids – Apply to Teach Kids English Online
Most online teachers will earn between $16-20/hr (USD) and work 10 – 20hrs per week. This includes both loyalty bonuses and wage growth.The majority of our opportunities are for teaching kids between ages 5 and 12. These are eager learners who bring a frequent smile to their teachers face.

iTutorGroup
iTutorGroup is the global leader in online education providing personalized learning experiences to hundreds of thousands of students and business professionals in countless subject matters through its network, and sourcing experts and teachers in thousands of centers, institutions and cities around the world. iTutorGroup does this by leveraging big data analytics and utilizing advanced algorithmic matching between students, classmates, teaching consultants and digital content. Since its inception in 1998, iTutorGroup has become the largest online platform driving live human-to-human interactions worldwide. iTutorGroup leads the revolution of education and live interaction with its human-to-human platform and service model. With iTutorGroup, anybody can learn anything from any device, anytime, 24-7.

Gogokid
We aspire to foster an environment conducive to education that will inspire young students in China to commit to a lifetime of learning. Our comprehensive and interactive platform connects enthusiastic and experienced teachers with eager students ready to explore their full potential.

English Hunt

Englishunt Inc. was founded in Seoul, Korea in December 2000 . Englishunt is an educational publisher with a focus on the creation of English education content. Englishunt Inc.'s business operations fall into two key areas: its product or content creation and distance education services.

Tutor.com

Tutor.com offers one-to-one learning solutions for students and professionals. All of our services are live, on demand and online. Homework help, tutoring, peer coaching, professional development, training, career help –we do it all. But it comes down to our core philosophy that when someone needs help the best way to get it is right away from an experienced expert. Our experts are online 24/7 ready to help. The results: over 14 million one-to-one sessions completed. 90% of the students, teachers, and professionals who use Tutor.com's services would recommend us to a friend.

Teach Away

From our beginnings as an international teacher recruitment startup, to launching our first professional development course for teachers, we've stayed true to our core mission: to create a world where every student experiences the power of a great teacher and realizes their full potential because of it.

MagicEars

Magic Ears is an innovative online English learning platform for students ages 4-12. With a relentless focus on the long-term, our mission is to bring a global classroom experience to every child and to provide the best online career opportunity for teachers.

Chegg Tutors

We'll send students to you, Log in when it's convenient for you to tutor. Build your reputation and get even more tutoring opportunities. Tutor from anywhereIn your dorm, coffee shop, or home all you need is internet access. Get paid each week focus on tutoring and we'll handle rates & billing.

TutorMe

TutorMe is a revolutionary online education platform that provides on-demand tutoring and online courses. We believe there are more teachers in the world than are actually teaching so we want to empower more people to learn from each other. Our platform enables thousands of tutors to share their knowledge with students around the globe. Whether you need help with high school algebra or you want to learn how to program in Python, we have a perfect tutor for you. At TutorMe, we want to change the way you learn.

Yup Homework Help Program

Yup is a mobile tutoring app that instantly connects students with expert tutors. Tutors help guide students through their problem by providing academic support, not answers.

Skooli

Our students want to learn from qualified educators like you. Convert your knowledge into cash and earn extra money in your spare time as a tutor. All you need is your expertise, a device, and a wifi connection. Skooli connects students with only the best online tutors, which is why our tutors are paid more than other online tutoring platforms. Start tutoring with Skooli and earn more.

Wyzant

One-to-one learning works. We've believed that from day one. But we also knew it would work better if it were accessible, affordable, and more convenient for everyone. So that's what we've built—an easier way to connect people who need to know with the experts that can teach them. And we've changed the way people think about education in the process.

Other Income Opportunities

Uber
On-demand transportation technology is our core service, and the app that connects driver-partners and riders is what makes it all possible.

Lyft
Rideshare with Lyft. Lyft is your friend with a car, whenever you need one. Download the app and get a ride from a friendly driver within minutes.

Lime | Electric Scooter Rentals, Micro Mobility Made Simple
Electric scooter rentals, e-assist bikes and pedal bikes for your city or campus. Micro-mobility for smart cities and universities. Download the Lime app!

Bird Scooters
Bird is a dockless scooter-share company based in Santa Monica, California. Founded in September 2017, Bird operates electric scooters in over 100 cities throughout North America, Europe, and Asia, with 10 million rides in its first year of operation.

Rover
Whether you need in-home dog boarding, pet sitting, dog walking, or day care, Rover connects pet parents with dog people who'll treat their pets like family.

Rover sitters are your rainy-day-dog-walkers. Your every-day-belly-rubbers. Your tug-of-war players. Your middle-of-the-night-pee-breakers. Because we get it—your dog is family. And when you can't be there, you can trust us to keep your dog happy, healthy, and sweet as ever.

But it's not just about dog love. Rover is also an award-winning technology business committed to making pet care safe, easy, and affordable so that everyone can experience the unconditional love of a dog.

Airbnb

Founded in 2008, Airbnb exists to create a world where anyone can belong anywhere, providing healthy travel that is local, authentic, diverse, inclusive and sustainable. Airbnb uniquely leverages technology to economically empower millions of people around the world to unlock and monetize their spaces, passions and talents to become hospitality entrepreneurs. Airbnb's accommodation marketplace provides access to 6+ million unique places to stay in more than 81,000 cities and 191 countries. With Experiences, Airbnb offers unprecedented access to local communities and interests through 25,000+ unique, handcrafted activities run by hosts across 1,000+ markets around the world. Airbnb's people-to-people platform benefits all its stakeholders, including hosts, guests, employees and the communities in which it operates.

VRBO   HomeAway.com   FlipKey

More Income Ideas

Additional Teaching opportunities, Recycling, bartend, Pet sitting/walking apps, donate plasma, wash cars, cut lawns, rake leaves, babysit, drop shipping, make YouTube videos, social media content, become an affiliate for your favorite websites (Ebay, Amazon are great!), House cleaning, clean Airbnb's, paid online surveys, Rent your car out using Turo, Sell the gift cards you never used online, sell things you aren't using around the house or up in the attic (Craigslist or FB Marketplace, Garage Sale) Use your talent (photography, teaching, music, graphic design, sewing, etc). Scroll under craigslist jobs. Make a social media post telling people you are looking to make some extra money if they know of any opportunities. There are infinite of ways to make more money. Be creative.

We will be launching an affiliate program that allows teachers who share our program to make a percentage of the sale – coming soon!

Student Loans

As stated in the Expense Eliminator Chapter, here are a few loan forgiveness programs for teachers. A complete list of state-based student loan forgiveness programs can be found at

www.debtfreeteacher.com/resources .

Teacher Loan Forgiveness | Federal Student Aid
This is the loan forgiveness program that I used. To qualify you must teach Math, Science, or SPED in a low-income based school (Title I) for 5 consecutive years. The program forgives $5,000-$17,500 depending on the grade level and if you are "highly qualified" or not. Once you have completed 5 years, you can apply for forgiveness.

Public Service Loan Forgiveness | Federal Student Aid
PSLF is one of the best ways to receive loan forgiveness. Teachers can receive complete Federal student loan forgiveness after 120 qualifying payments (10yrs). This program is awesome because it is applicable for any teacher at any school.

Perkins Loan Cancellation and Discharge | Federal Student Aid
If you have Perkins Loans, you can see your entire loan balance forgiven over 5 years. The great thing about this program is that it gives forgiveness in increments, so even if you don't make it

5 years, you can at least see some of your loan balance disappear. Private schools can be eligible. You must teach math, science, foreign language, bilingual studies, and any other content area that has been determined to be in shortage in your state.

Contact

If this book helped you in anyway, be sure to leave a review. The Facebook group is a great place to meet others who are going through the same journey as you. Please stop in and ask questions, share your story, and join the discussion.

Email: info@debtfreeteachers.com

Website: www.debtfreeteacher.com

Instagram:@the.debt.free.teacher

FB Group: www.facebook.com/groups/debtfreeteacher

FB Page: www.facebook.com/debtfreeteacher

www.ingramcontent.com/pod-product-compliance
Lightning Source LLC
LaVergne TN
LVHW041237080426
835508LV00011B/1251